1.   Introduction

The Twenty-first Amendment repealed prohibition, but granted the states power to regulate the sale of alcohol to consumers. Pursuant to this authority, states have set up a collection of regulations that limit the ability of beer, wine, and liquor producers to control the distribution of their product. Almost every state has mandated a "three-tier" distribution system, which requires an alcohol producer (or licensed importer) to sell their products to a wholesale distributor, and those wholesale distributors, in turn, to sell to the products to retailers, who in turn, sell the products to final consumers. There are a variety of state regulations of alcohol distribution that interact within the three-tier system.

Many states also have enacted franchise protection laws, which make it extraordinarily difficult for suppliers to terminate their contractual relationships with wholesalers.[1] These laws typically prohibit the termination of wholesaler except for "just cause," and set up elaborate administrative processes for proving "just cause."[2] Franchise protection laws may require that a demonstration of "good cause" include revocation of a wholesaler's license; bankruptcy or receivership of the wholesaler; assignment for the benefit of creditors of the wholesaler's assets; or failure of the wholesaler "to substantially comply" with a "reasonable and material requirement imposed upon him in writing."[3]

Further, several states have enacted laws that require alcohol producers to grant exclusive geographic territories to their distributors, which exacerbate the problems that "just cause" laws create by preventing a producer from simply hiring another distributor in the same territory to distribute its brand in competition with the non-performing incumbent distributor. Still others prohibit exclusive dealing arrangements between a producer and a distributor. There is a vast economics literature which

---

[1] See, e.g., NMSA 1978 § 60-8A-8 ("The purpose of [the franchise termination laws] is to provide an equal bargaining position between the parties and to protect the health, safety and welfare of the citizens by ensuring that there is an orderly and fair distribution of alcoholic beverages in the state.").

[2] See, e.g., VA Code § 4.1-406 ("Notwithstanding the terms, provisions or conditions of any agreement, no winery shall unilaterally amend, cancel, terminate or refuse to renew any agreement, or unilateral cause a wholesaler to resign from an agreement, unless the winery has first [required notice to terminate] and good cause exists for the amendment . . ..").

[3] Id.

1

explores the competitive effects of these state restrictions of alcohol distribution and of contractual relationships between alcohol producers and distributors. This literature provides evidence that generally supports the conclusion that these state regulations are associated with harm to consumers in the form of higher prices and reduced output.[4]

One of the most potentially harmful state alcohol distribution regulations are "post and hold" laws ("PH laws"). Although there is some variation in the substance of PH laws, they generally require that alcohol distributors "post" their proposed prices in advance, thus sharing future prices with rival distributors before they go into effect, and then "hold" these prices for a specified period of time. From a competition policy perspective, PH laws have the potential to harm consumers in two ways. First, PH laws may facilitate tacit or explicit collusion among distributions. Second, PH laws may also diminish unilateral incentives to engage in price-cutting. In both cases, consumers pay higher prices. This danger has led several federal courts of appeals to strike down PH laws as unconstitutionally in conflict with federal antitrust laws. In response to these and other legal challenges to state alcohol regulations, Congress is currently considering legislation that would hinder plaintiffs' ability to challenge PH laws, including introducing a requirement that any such plaintiff must prove by clear and convincing evidence "that the law has no effect on the promotion of temperance, the establishment or maintenance of orderly alcoholic beverage markets, the collection of beverage taxes, the structure of the state alcoholic beverage distribution system, or the restriction of access to alcoholic beverages by those under the legal drinking age."[5]

The key policy questions concerning PH laws, and state regulation of alcohol more broadly, turn on an empirical examination of both their competitive and social effects. In this paper, we investigate both the effect of PH laws on alcohol consumption as well as whether PH laws reduce some of the well-known social costs associated with consumption. Using a panel of 50 states from 1983-2004, we find that PH laws are associated with lower levels of consumer consumption of beer, wine, and spirits. Specifically, consumers in states with PH laws consume between 2-8 percent less

---

[4] *See, e.g.*, Sass (2005); Sass & Saurman (1993, 1996); Slade (1988).

[5] Comprehensive Alcohol Regulatory Effectiveness (CARE) Act, H.R. 5034, 111th Cong. (2010), *available at* http://frwebgate.access.gpo.gov/cgi-bin/getdoc.cgi?dbname=111_cong_bills&docid=f:h5034ih.txt.pdf.

alcohol (measured in ethanol equivalent gallons), with the effects for wine and spirits relatively larger than those for beer. These results generally are robust to the inclusion of state and time effects, national and state-specific linear trends, and techniques to control for the possible endogeneity of PH laws. The results are consistent with the prior literature linking state regulation of the alcoholic beverage industry to consumer harm in the form of lower output and higher prices. These results are further consistent with the underlying economics of PH laws, which increase incentives to collude and decrease unilateral incentives to discount. While we find that PH laws have a predictably negative impact on alcohol consumption, we also find that PH laws have no measurable effect on drunk driving accidents and various measures of teen drinking. On the other hand, laws that directly target drunk driving and underage drinking appear to reduce these behaviors. Together, our results cast serious doubt on the wisdom of any legislative attempts to increase the difficulty of mounting antitrust challenges to PH laws, since successful antitrust suits are likely to improve consumer welfare.

The remainder of the paper is organized as follows. Section 2 provides a brief overview of the law and economics of PH laws. Section 3 presents the results of our analysis of the impact of PH laws on output and Section 4 presents the results of our analysis concerning PH laws and social harms. Section 5 discusses the policy implications of our results and Section 6 concludes.

2.   The Law & Economics of Post-and-Hold Laws

PH laws impose two general requirements on wholesalers: they must "post" their prices for the coming period with a state authority responsible for regulating alcohol sales, and they most "hold" these prices for the duration of the period. For example, New York's PH law requires beer, wine, and spirits wholesalers to file by the fifth day of each month the prices that they intend to charge the following month.[6] New York wholesalers must hold these prices for the following month.[7] Hold periods vary, with some states mandating longer hold periods for price reductions than for price

---

[6] *See* NY Alc. Bev. Con. § 101-b; NY Alc. Bev. Con. § 55-b.

[7] *Id.*

increases.[8] Some PH laws also make planned future prices available to competing wholesalers and allow wholesalers to adjust their posted prices downward. Again, New York law makes posted prices available to competitors ten days after they are filed and allows wholesalers three business days to adjust their prices to meet lower competing prices.[9] For example, a New York wholesaler would files its prices for July on June 5. On June 15, the state would make these prices available to all wholesalers, who would have until June 18 to change their postings to meet lower prices. The prices posted on June 18 would then be in effect for July.

As shown in Table 1, nineteen states have adopted PH laws since 1983. Currently ten states have PH laws applying to wine wholesalers,[10] nine states have PH laws applying to beer wholesalers,[11] and nine states have PH laws applying to spirit wholesalers.[12] Since 1983, seven states have repealed their PH laws, primarily as a result of court decisions.[13]

2.1 Coordinated and Unilateral Effects

Economics has long stressed the role of communication in facilitating collusion; absent credible information on each others' actions, it becomes difficult for rival firms to coordinate.[14] PH laws make coordinated pricing among wholesalers more likely by making it easier for competing firms to reach and enforce agreements on prices.

As a threshold matter, firms must be able to agree on a price for collusion to work. When the proverbial "smoke-filled-room" is unavailable to facilitate agreement, firms must find other means to coordinate their actions. Heterogeneous firms are likely

---

[8] For example, Idaho has a 30-day hold period for price increases, but a 180-day hold period for price decreases. *See* IC §§, 23-1029; 23-1329.

[9] *Id.* Connecticut, Missouri, and Oklahoma PH laws have similar provisions, as did the Maryland and Massachusetts PH laws before they were repealed.

[10] CT, ID, ME, MI, MO, NJ, NY, OK, SD, and WA.

[11] CT, GA, ID, ME, MI, NJ, OK, TN, and WA.

[12] CT, GA, MI, MO, NJ, NY, OK, SD, and WV.

[13] DE (1999), MD (2004), MA (1998), NB (1984), OR (1990), PA (1999) and WA (2008).

[14] Kühn (2001) ("The notion that communication is central to collusion is without doubt part of the general folklore of competition policy at least going back to Adam Smith."); Stigler (1964); Albaek et al. (1997) ("At least since Stigler's seminal article, [industrial organization] literature has stressed the importance for (tacitly) colluding oligopolists of observing firm-specific transactions prices of their rivals and rapidly detecting changes in these. Otherwise, collusion is prone to break down.").

to have different ideal collusive price points. Thus, even if firms all want to collude, if they cannot communicate which prices they prefer, collusion may nonetheless be impossible. Announcement of future prices can help solve the coordination problem by providing a focal point for cartel members, thus reducing strategic uncertainty and making collusion more likely.[15] That PH laws require wholesalers to charge the prices they announce, moreover, converts what may otherwise be "cheap talk" into a credible commitment, further increasing the probability that firms will be able to coordinate their pricing decisions.[16] PH laws also provide wholesalers with an accurate record of past prices, which can help facilitate future coordination.[17]

Second, as a general matter, collusive schemes can be maintained as long as the present value from adhering to the price-fixing agreement is greater than the benefits from cheating.[18] The likelihood that this condition will hold, in turn, depends positively on the extent to which cartel members can detect deviations and punish them with intense competition.[19] By requiring wholesalers to share their prices with competitors prior to them going into effect, post-and-hold regulations can make detection easier. Further, wholesalers are legally required to refrain from offering discounts off their posted prices during the hold period, which decreases the likelihood of cheating. Post-and-hold regimes that allow competitors to adjust prices after seeing competitors pricing, but before they go into effect, moreover, reduce the expected gains from cheating because the cartel members can punish competition before the cheater enjoys any market share gains.

---

[15] *See* Vives (2002); Kühn (2001); Møllgaard & Overgaard (2001).

[16] Announcement of future prices or other strategic decisions that are non-binding, or so-called "cheap talk," is less likely to enable collusion than a binding announcement. In some circumstances, however, cheap talk can enhance the probability of successful collusion relative to no communication at all. *See* Farrell (1987); *see also* Doyle & Snyder (1999) (finding evidence that automakers respond strategically to production announcements by rivals); Gillespie (1995) (describing how non-committal pre announcement of airline fares facilitated collusion among airline members).

[17] *See* Green & Porter (1984).

[18] Tirole (1988, at 245-57).

[19] For example, in a dynamic Cournot oligopoly model firms may agree to charge something between the Cournot price and the monopoly price during collusive periods and then to charge the Cournot price to punish deviations. Green & Porter (1984).

Consistent with the notion that sharing pricing information among competitors may soften competition, several studies have found positive correlations between policies that publicized previously private contracts and higher prices. For example, Albaek et al. (1997) study the Danish ready-mix concrete industry and find that after the government forced publication of negotiated prices, average prices rose by as much as 25 percent, and firms began to discontinue large discounts off list price.[20] Other studies have found that forced disclosure of negotiated prices is associated with higher prices in railroad markets.[21] In addition, some experimental evidence suggests that communication (even cheap talk) among players in non-cooperative games can shift prices from competitive levels toward monopoly levels.[22]

Further, antitrust cases in the US have focused on information sharing as a means to facilitate collusion.[23] For example, the Department of Justice sued eight major airlines and the Airline Tariff Publishing Company (ATP), alleging that the airlines used the ATP to exchange information about future prices via the ATP to facilitate a price-fixing agreement.[24] Several courts, moreover, have found that PH laws mimic agreements between rival wholesalers to hold prices, which constitute *per se* illegal conduct under the Sherman Act.[25] In one case, for example, a wholesaler testified that he and rival wholesalers used the public posting to reach an agreement on a new price for beer. According to the court:

> Maletis testified that in 1986 . . . his wholesale business and one of the largest beer and wine wholesalers in the State of Oregon, used the price posting exchange at the OLCC as a starting point for communicating with

---

[20] *See* Albaek et al., *supra* note 14, at 440.

[21] *See* Fuller et al. (1990); Schmitz & Fuller (1995). Other studies have found evidence to suggest that rivals in the automobile and paper industries respond strategically to each other's announced plans of future production and capacity expansion. See Doyle & Snyder, *supra* note 16; Christensen & Caves (1997).

[22] *See* Kühn, *supra* note 14, at 82-83 for a summary of this evidence.

[23] The EC and its member states also have focused enforcement attention on various information sharing regimes. *See* Møllgaard & Overgaard, *supra* note 15, at 112-21 (discussing information sharing cases in Europe involving wood pulp, tractors, and gasoline).

[24] Specifically the airlines allegedly would use the ATP to suggest future collusive prices for routes that could be withdrawn if no agreement was reached. Further, the airlines allegedly used the ATP to threaten punishments for deviations. *See* Gillespie (1995); Viscusi et al. (2005).

[25] *See* pages 7-11, *infra*, and accompany text.

competing wholesalers of keg beer until agreement was reach by all wholesalers of keg beer on a new wholesale price for keg beer. [26]

PH laws also provide firms with unilateral incentives to soften wholesale price competition by making price cuts more expensive. In settings where parties negotiate individual contracts and differential pricing is allowed, sellers will offer secret discounts to attract marginal buyers. Policies that force sellers to offer the same price to all buyers reduce incentives to discount because the discount must be offered to both marginal and inframarginal buyers. For example, "most-favored customer" (MFC) regulations, which require sellers to offer their lowest negotiated price to all buyers, have been shown to lead to higher overall price levels in some market settings. [27] Further, wholesalers also may have less incentive to offer discounts when their competitors can match them instantaneously. The gain from offering a discount to a retailer is increased sales of that brand. When discounts are made public, and are announced to all rivals before going into effect, competing wholesalers can offer the same discount, diluting market share gains from price cuts. Finally, holding requirements make price reductions more expensive by forcing wholesalers to commit to them for extended periods of time. The holding requirement also constrains wholesalers' ability to experiment with price reductions; this effect is likely to be especially pronounced in PH regimes that have longer holding requirements for price reductions than for price increases. Further, longer sale periods expose wholesalers to risks in supply or demand changes, thus further increasing their costs.

2.2   Antitrust Treatment of PH Laws

---

[26] *See Miller v. Hedlund,* 717 F. Supp. 711, 714 (D. Ore. 1989).

[27] *See e.g.,* Scott-Morton (1997) (finding evidence that MFC rules that required pharmaceutical companies to offer their lowest price to Medicaid purchasers led to higher average drug prices in some categories). Private adoption of MFC clauses between providers and insurers has raised competitive issues in some circumstances. *See e.g., U.S. v. Delta Dental of Rhode Island,* 943 F.Supp. 172 (D. RI. 1996) (denying defendant's motion to dismiss antitrust complaint alleging dental insurer's MFC clauses with participating dentist violated Sherman § 1); *but see Blue Cross & Blue Shield United of Wisconsin v. Marshfield Clinic,* 65 F.3d 1406 (7th Cir. 1995) (finding no evidence that MFC clauses between an insurer and providers were anticompetitive); *Ocean state Physicians Health Plan, Inc. v. Blue Cross & Blue Shield of Rhode Island,* 883 F.2d 1101 (1st Cir. 1989) (upholding JNOV finding MFC clauses between insurer and providers did not violate Sherman § 2). For a discussion of the competition issues surrounding MFC clauses *see* Baker (1996). *See also* Salop (1986).

7

In general, the "state action doctrine" provides states immunity from antitrust scrutiny when they replace competition with a system of regulation.[28] States, however, cannot authorize private individuals to violate the federal antitrust laws. Thus, federal antitrust laws will preempt state regulatory schemes that permit (or compel) private parties to engage in conduct that would otherwise constitute a *per se* violation of the Sherman Act.[29] Because PH laws create conditions that are likely to facilitate coordinated pricing, it should not be surprising that these laws have been challenged as being in direct conflict with the Sherman Act. Although not every challenge to PH laws has succeeded, the weight of authority suggests that the federal antitrust laws preempt these schemes.

For example in the two most recent preemption challenges, the Fourth and Ninth Circuits struck down PH laws. The Fourth Circuit addressed the validity of Maryland PH laws in *TFWS, Inc. v. Schaefer*,[30] and engaged in a two-step antitrust analysis: (1) do the state's pricing regulations violate the Sherman Act? and (2) if so, are they nevertheless protected by the state action doctrine?[31] With regard to the first step, the court further bifurcated the analysis to determine (a) whether the restraint is "unilateral" or "hybrid," (b) if it is a hybrid, whether it involves a *per se* violation of Sherman § 1.[32] The court ultimately concluded that Maryland's PH scheme "was a classic hybrid restraint: the State requires wholesalers to set prices and stick to them, but it does not review those privately set prices for reasonableness; the wholesalers are thus granted a significant degree of private regulatory power."[33] The Fourth Circuit also found that by mandating adherence to an announced price, Maryland's law effectively required *per se* illegal price fixing.[34] Finally, the court held that the law was

---

[28] *See Parker v. Brown*, 317 U.S. 341 (1943); *Cal. Retail Liquor Dealers Ass'n v. Midcal Aluminum, Inc.*, 445 U.S. 91 (1980).

[29] *See* Cooper & Kovacic (2010), for a more detailed discussion of the antitrust preemption doctrine.

[30] 242 F.3d 198 (4th Cir. 2001).

[31] *Id.* at 206.

[32] *Id.* at 207.

[33] *Id.* at 208-09.

[34] *Id.* at 209 (citing *Catalano, Inc.* 446 U.S. at 649-50 and *Sugar Institute v. United States*, 297 U.S. 553, 581 (1936))

not immune under the state action doctrine because although the PH scheme was pursuant to clearly articulated policy, Maryland failed to "actively supervise" the resulting prices.[35] The Ninth Circuit's decision in *Costco Wholesale Corp. v. Maleng*[36] is the most recent appellate decision implicating the legality of PH laws. The court followed the framework from *TFWS*,[37] and found Washington's PH law to be a hybrid restraint[38] and to constitute a *per se* violation of the Sherman Act because it closely mimicked an agreement among competitors to adhere to posted prices.[39] Accordingly, the Ninth Circuit upheld the district court's ruling that the Sherman Act preempted Washington's PH law.[40]

2.3   The Twenty-first Amendment

Even if an alcohol regulation is preempted by the federal antitrust laws, it nevertheless may be a valid exercise of the state's power under the Twenty-first Amendment. As noted above, section two of the Twenty-first Amendment gives states control over the "transportation and importation" of alcohol within their borders,[41] and the Supreme Court has interpreted this Constitutional provision as granting states

---

[35] *Id.* at 211.

[36] 522 F.3d 874 (9th Cir. 2008).

[37] *Id.* at 888 (expressing doubt as to whether the hybrid inquiry was any different than the active supervision inquiry under *Midcal* and stating that "Until the Supreme Court further clarifies this doctrinally confusing area, however, we will follow the lead of other courts and begin by determining whether the restraint is hybrid or unilateral").

[38] *Id.* at 894.

[39] *Id.* at 895.

[40] The result in *Costco* is similar to that in an earlier Ninth Circuit PH law case, *Miller v. Hedlund*, 813 F.2d 1344 (9th Cir. 1987). There, the court noted that although mere agreements to exchange pricing information are not *per se* illegal, the court noted that "agreement[s] to adhere to previously announced prices and terms of sale" are. *Id.* at 1348-49 (citing *Catalano, Inc. v. Target Sales, Inc.*, 446 U.S. 643 (1980)). The court held that conduct pursuant to Oregon's PH law constituted a *per se* violation of the Sherman Act. Having found that the PH law was subject to preemption, the *Hedlund* court quickly dispensed of it by holding that Oregon did not adequately supervise the resulting prices. *Id.* at 1348. In *Battipaglia v. New York State Liquor Authority*, 745 F.2d 166 (2d Cir. 1984), the Second Circuit found that the Sherman Act did not reach New York post-and-hold regulations. The court noted disagreement among courts as to whether the conduct mandated by the PH law could satisfy the agreement element of Sherman § 1, but declined to decide the issue. Rather, it assumed *arguendo* that an agreement could be found, but ultimately held the PH law was not preempted because mere information exchanges among competitors are not *per se* illegal. *Id.* at 175

[41] U.S. CONST. amend. XXI, § 2.

virtually complete power to structure their liquor distribution system.[42] At the same time, however, the Court has been clear that Congress used the full extent of its power to regulate interstate commerce when it enacted the federal antitrust laws, which embodied a national policy in favor of free-market competition.[43] Further, the Court has been equally clear that a state's power to regulate alcohol sales within its border is not absolute and must yield to Congress's Commerce Clause power in some circumstances.[44] Thus, even in circumstances where the Sherman Act preempts a regulatory scheme, a court still must determine whether in that particular circumstance the state's constitutionally protected right to regulate alcohol within their borders nevertheless trumps Congress' commerce power, which defines the reach of the antitrust laws.

In *Cal. Retail Dealers Ass'n v. Midcal Aluminum* and *324 Liquor Corp. v. Duffy*, the Court set out a broad framework to weigh these competing interests, asking "whether the interest implicated by a state regulation are so closely related to the powers reserved by the Twenty-first Amendment that the regulation may prevail, notwithstanding that its requirements directly conflict with express federal policies."[45] In both cases, moreover, the Court noted that the state must substantiate, rather than merely assert, the nexus between the regulatory scheme and its Twenty-first Amendment interests.[46] More recently, the Fourth and Ninth Circuit have imposed

---

[42] *Cal. Retail Dealers Ass'n v. Midcal Aluminum*, 445 U.S. at 110 ("The Twenty-first Amendment grants the States virtually complete control over whether to permit importation or sale of liquor and how to structure the liquor distribution system.").

[43] *See Midcal,* 445 U.S. at 111 (Congress "exercis[ed] all the power it possessed under the Commerce clause when it approved the Sherman Act."); *City of Lafayette v. Lousiana Power & Light Co.*, 435 U.S. 389, 398 (1978) (by enacting the Sherman Act, "Congress, exercising the full extent of its constitutional power, sought to establish a regime of competition as the fundamental principle governing commerce in this country").

[44] *See Granholm v. Heald,* 544 U.S. 460, 487 (2005) ("the court has held that § 2 does no abrogate Congress' Commerce Clause powers with regard to liquor"); *Capital Cities Cable, Inc. v. Crisp*, 467 U.S. 691, 713 (1984) ("Notwithstanding the [Twenty-first] Amendment's broad grant of power to the States, . . . the Federal Government plainly retains authority under the Commerce Clause to regulate even interstate commerce in liquor"); *Midcal*, 445 U.S. at 110 ("Although States retain substantial discretion to establish other liquor regulations, those controls may be subject to the federal commerce power in appropriate situations."); *Duffy*, 479 U.S. at 346 ("The States' Twenty-first Amendment powers, though broad, are circumscribed by other provisions of the Constitution.").

[45] *Duffy*, 479 U.S. at 347.

[46] *See Midcal*, 445 U.S. at 114; *Duffy*, 479 U.S. at 350.

additional structure onto this inquiry, articulating the following three-step inquiry: (1) whether the expressed state interest one protected by the Twenty-first Amendment, (2) whether the regulatory scheme effectively serves this purpose, and (3) assuming the first two questions are answered in the affirmative, whether those state interests are sufficient to prevail against the federal interest in promoting competition through the antitrust laws.[47]

The range of interests implicated by the Twenty-first Amendment has never been definitively identified, but courts have recognized promoting temperance[48] and preventing price discrimination[49] as legitimate Twenty-first Amendment objectives. It is unclear whether protecting small retailers is a Twenty-first Amendment concern.[50] In an intergovernmental immunity case, moreover, the Supreme Court has stated in dicta that raising revenues and ensuring "orderly market conditions" also were core interests under the Twenty-first Amendment.[51] In another Twenty-first Amendment case, the Eleventh Circuit, however, remarked more recently on the amorphousness of this concept: "As for 'ensuring orderly markets,' we are not sure what that phrase means."[52]

The second step, assessing the efficacy of the regulation in promoting the asserted goal, is a fact-intensive inquiry. The state bears the burden of demonstrating that its regulatory scheme actually affects the state's asserted Twenty-first Amendment

---

[47] *See Costco*, 522 F.3d at 902; *TFWS*, 242 F.3d at 213.

[48] *See Midcal*, 445 U.S. at 112; *Duffy*, 479 U.S. at 349; *Costco*, 522 F.3d at 902 ("We have no doubt that . . . temperance was a valid and important interest of the State under the Twenty-first Amendment."); *TFWS*, 242 F.2d at 213 (noting "the Twenty-first Amendment definitely allows a state to promote temperance").

[49] *Miller v. Hedlund*, 717 F. Supp. 711, 715 (D. Ore. 1989).

[50] Although the Supreme Court entertained this rationale in both *Midcal* and *Duffy*, it was careful to say in both cases that it was deciding the cases based on the lack of demonstrated nexus between the regulatory scheme and the protection of small retailers. Thus, it was not required to reach the issue of whether protecting small retailers "ever could prevail against the federal interest in enforcement of antitrust laws." *Duffy*, 479 U.S. at 350 n.12; *see also Midcal*, 445 U.S. at 113-14.

[51] *North Dakota v. United States*, 495 U.S. 423, 432 (1990). In *Midcal*, the Supreme Court appeared to accept the California Supreme Court's interpretation of "orderly markets" to mean protection of small retailers, but did not consider whether such protection is a legitimate Twenty-first Amendment interest.

[52] *Bainbridge v. Turner*, 311 F.3d 1104, 1115 (11th Cir. 2002). *See also Costco*, 522 F.3d. at 1429 n. 23 (

11

interests.[53] For example, in both *Midcal* and *Duffy*, the Supreme Court relied on state court evidentiary findings that both regulatory schemes were ineffective at protecting retailers and reducing drinking. In *Costco*, moreover, despite evidence that Washington has one of the lowest per capita alcohol consumption rates in the country, the Ninth Circuit upheld the district court's holding that the state could not satisfy its burden at this step because it failed to demonstrate a link between moderation and the regulatory scheme.[54] Further, in *TFWS*, the Fourth Circuit found the district court's assumption that higher prices led to lower consumption insufficient for this inquiry and remanded to develop an evidentiary record on the relationship between the state's restrictions on competition and their purported Twenty-first Amendment goals. Underscoring the fact-intensive nature of the inquiry at this step, the district court ultimately found against the state,[55] but the resolution required two additional trips to the Fourth Circuit to address methodological issues.[56] Because states defending PH laws have failed at steps one and two in the Twenty-first Amendment test, there is no indication of how courts would perform the third-step balancing of interests.

3.   The Effect of PH Laws on Alcohol Consumption

We begin by examining the impact of PH laws on output to measure their competitive impact. If, as economic theory predicts, PH laws weaken incentives for wholesalers to compete, they will raise alcohol prices and reduce consumption. Of course, regulation that reduces alcohol consumption can produce social benefits – it is well established that alcohol is associated with a host of social harms, ranging from drunk driving to domestic violence and property crime. To preview, after showing a

---

[53] *See Costco*, 522 F.3d at 902 (noting that the answer to the second part of the test "may ultimately rest upon findings and conclusions having a large factual component.") (quoting *Miller*, 813 F.2d at 1352).

[54] *See id.*

[55] *TFWS, Inc. v. Schaefer*, 2007 WL 2917025 (D. Md. Sept. 27, 2007).

[56] *See TFWS, Inc. v. Schaefer*, 147 Fed. Appx. 330, 2005 WL 1898273 (4th Cir. Oct. 5, 2005); *TFWS, Inc. v. Schaefer*, 325 F.3d 234 (4th Cir. 2003). A paradox that seemingly emerges from this second inquiry is that the more anticompetitive the regulation, the more likely it is to pass Twenty-first Amendment muster. For example, in *TFWS*, if the state were able reliably to show that its PH laws led to higher prices in Maryland than in Delaware, or that the regulations in *Midcal* and *Duffy* reduced alcohol consumption, the outcome may have been different. Similarly, the outcome of the Twenty-first Amendment inquiries in *Midcal* and *Duffy* may have changed had the evidence introduced in the lower courts revealed the regulatory schemes to protect small businesses from competition.

robust negative relationship between PH laws and alcohol consumption in this section, we next examine the extent to which PH laws generate any offsetting benefits in the form of reduced social harms. Specifically, we focus our attention on alcohol-related accidents and underage drinking and find no measurable relationship between PH laws and these social harms. Taken together, our results suggest that any social benefits from PH laws are likely to be very small, which is consistent with the measured reduction in consumption occurring primarily in the segment of the population that is not likely to engage in the harmful behavior that we examine.

3.1   Data and Methodology

We examine changes in alcohol consumption to identify the effects of PH laws on competition. If PH laws create incentives for wholesalers to raise prices – either unilaterally or via tacit or express collusion – alcohol consumption should fall. In what follows, we estimate various specifications of the following equation:

$$A_{i,t} = c + \alpha_i + \delta_t + \beta_1 PH_{i,t} + \beta_2 \mathbf{X}_{i,t} + e_{i,t}, \qquad (1)$$

where $A_{i,t}$ is alcohol consumption, PH is a dummy variable equal to 1 if state i had a PH law in effect at time t, and α_i and δ_t are state and year effects, respectively, and $\mathbf{X}_{i,t}$ is a vector of exogenous explanatory variables. We estimate separate regressions for per capita (based on state populations ages 14 and older) consumption of beer, wine, spirits, and all alcoholic beverages (in ethanol equivalent gallons) as reported by the National Institute on Alcohol Abuse and Alcoholism, part of the National Institutes of Health.[57] X includes controls for additional variables that are likely to be related to alcohol consumption or to unobserved heterogeneity correlated with both alcohol consumption and the presence of a PH law. Specifically, this vector includes real median household income per capita and the percentage of the population that are, respectively: younger than age 18, married, white, Evangelical, and Catholic. Demographic data come from the Census and religion data come from the Association of Religion Data Archive. The X vector also includes two variables that are correlated with price – an important determinant of consumption – but may reasonably be treated as exogenous: real total

---

[57]Available at:
http://www.niaaa.nih.gov/Resources/DatabaseResources/QuickFacts/AlcoholSales/consum03.htm.

alcohol taxation measured in dollars per gallon;[58] and for the wine and spirits regressions, a measure of the Herfindahl-Hirschman Index (HHI) for wine and spirit wholesaler concentration.[59] We also include variables that indicate the presence of certain state laws that may reduce alcohol consumption: a minimum legal drinking age of 21 (MLDA21); zero tolerance laws, (ZT), which lower the legal blood alcohol content for drivers under 21 to zero; and laws that lowered the permissible adult blood alcohol content from .10 to .08 (BAC08). Inclusion of these variables also provides symmetry with the social harms regressions in the next section. These data span 1983-2004. Descriptive statistics are shown in Table 2.

3.2   Results

Table 3 presents the main results for the full sample estimated in logs for ease of interpretation.[60] The first column reports the baseline regressions with only time and state effects, which show that PH laws are associated with lower alcohol consumption, although only the coefficients on wine and total consumption are significant. The second column includes demographic variables and proxies for price. The estimated PH coefficients remain negative, but now beer and spirits PH laws have larger and statistically significant effects on consumption (-.04 and -.10, respectively). The third column adds controls for religion, and all PH law estimates remain negative and significant. Further, that the estimated coefficients on Evangelical and Catholic generally take on negative and positive signs (although often insignificant), respectively, is consistent with the respective stances that these religious groups took on prohibition.[61] Column 4 includes indicator dummies for the adoption of laws aimed directly at alcohol consumption and drunk driving. The estimated effects of PH laws remain negative and significant in these specifications, and the estimated effects of MLDA21, ZT, and BAC08 (not reported) are generally negative but insignificant. It is

---

[58] This variable is calculated by summing state excise taxes and percentage markups converted to dollar amounts per gallon based on the American Chamber of Commerce Research Association (ACCRA) prices for wine, beer, and liquor for a given state.

[59] The authors are grateful to Michelle Mullins for providing these data, collected from the Adams Wine Handbook (various years).

[60] Linear specifications generate qualitatively similar results. Coefficient estimates for X variables are in the appendix.

[61] See DANIEL OKRENT, LAST CALL (2010). Coefficient estimates for tax, HHI, and religion variables from various specifications are in the Appendix.

not surprising that BAC.08 and ZT are not linked to lower levels of consumption, as these policies were targeted directly at drunk driving. That MLDA21 is insignificant is likely due to the lack of intrastate variation in the sample; by 1983, the first year of the sample, all but 4 states had adopted a 21 year drinking age, and all had adopted by 1988.

Alcohol consumption – especially spirit consumption – was declining generally over the first half of the sample period. To control for any trend in unobserved tastes for alcohol Columns 5 and 6 report the results from specifications with linear national and state-specific trends, respectively. With the addition of the national trend, results remain largely unchanged in terms of magnitudes and significance. The addition of state-specific trends, however, causes the PH law coefficients to fall by around half for spirits and all alcohol, although these coefficients remain significant. The estimated effect of PH laws on wine consumption, however, changes signs and become statistically indistinguishable from zero. An examination of the trend coefficients suggests that the wine series is not trended. The national trend is negative and significant for beer, spirits, and all beverages, but positive and insignificant for wine. Similarly, although most of the state-specific trends are negative and significant for beer, spirits, and all beverages, they are either positive or statistically indistinguishable from zero for wine. Absent a trend to pick up, the correlation between state-specific trends, state effects, PH laws, and other right-hand-side variables may make it difficult to detect any PH law effect.

Table 4 presents results from estimating various specifications of (1) after removing control states – those states that take full control of distribution of certain types of alcohol – from the sample. The rationale for this approach is to ensure that the results are not attributable to systematic differences between alcohol consumption in control and license states that may bias the estimates. The results remain essentially the same in terms of magnitude and statistical significance. As with the full sample, once state-specific linear trends are added, the PH law effect falls for each type of drink and becomes insignificant for wine. The standard error of the estimate on all beverages increases, causing it to also become insignificant at standard levels.

The estimate of $\hat{\beta}_1$ is identified from within-state variation of the PH law treatment, and the source of this variation for all but two states (Washington adopting a PH law in 1995 and Delaware abandoning in 1999[62]) was the elimination of PH laws resulting from a court ruling rather than legislative action. Accordingly, it seems reasonable to view PH law treatment as exogenous. Nonetheless, as a final robustness check, we also control for the possibility that the PH law treatment is correlated with unobserved state-level heterogeneity that determines alcohol consumption. It could be the case, for example, that populations with underlying preferences for alcohol are more likely to repeal PH laws to make consumption cheaper. Such a correlation would bias $\hat{\beta}_1$ downward, possibly leading to the false inference regarding the causal relationship between PH laws and lower alcohol consumption.[63] We take two approaches to address this potential endogeneity problem.

First, we focus our analysis exclusively on those states that have adopted PH laws. If underlying preferences correlated with tastes for alcohol consumption lead to PH law adoption in the first place, a focus on these states should help control for endogeneity. Column 1 of Table 5 reports results of the full model with this limited sample and shows that PH laws are associated with lower consumption of each type of alcoholic beverage and all beverages combined. Once state-specific trends are introduced, however, PH laws appear to have a significant effect only on beer consumption, and weakly significant effect on all beverages. Column 2 focuses more narrowly on a subset of Northeastern states. Delaware and Massachusetts abandoned wine and beer PH laws in1998 and 1999, respectively. That these states are geographically contiguous is likely to further address possible confounding unobservable variables. In the model without state-specific trends, the estimated PH coefficients remain negative and statistically significant, although the magnitude for spirits and wine falls by about half. When state trends are introduced, however, all

---

[62] It is possible, however, that the amendments to Delaware's requirements were driven by contemporaneous adverse court decisions regarding PH laws in Massachusetts and Pennsylvania.

[63] Of course, if states that have relatively high alcohol consumption are more likely to adopt PH laws – for example, in an attempt to temper consumption or to collect taxes and rents on high levels of consumption – the bias would go in the opposite direction, which implies that the current estimates are conservative.

estimated PH law effects fall in magnitude so that none are statistically distinguishable from zero. In fact, the state-specific trends are significant in only three instances and with the exception of the tax and evangelical effects in the spirits regression, none of the right-hand-side variables in any regression are significant once state-specific trends are introduced. That the introduction of state-specific trends in small samples with errors clustered at the state level leads to insignificance is not surprising. Clustering essentially reduces the number of independent observations from 174 to 7 (number of states in the sample). Further, state trends are collinear with fixed effects and other exogenous variables, so it may be asking too much of the data to distinguish between the consumption effects of PH laws, state-specific trends, state effects, time effects, and other right-hand-side covariates with so few observations and groups.[64]

We also directly control for the possibility that the PH law treatment is correlated with the error term in (1) by estimating an endogenous treatment model. We model the probability that state i has adopted a PH law at time t as a function of the percent of Democratic legislators in a state legislature and the state tobacco excise tax rate. Assuming that Democratic law makers are more likely to favor regulation than their Republican counterparts, and that states with high tobacco taxes are likely to favor policies that enhance the ability to tax alcohol (for revenue or paternalistic purposes), these variables should be associated with higher probabilities of adopting a PH law. We use maximum likelihood to jointly estimate the first-stage selection probit and equation (1).[65] Results with and without the inclusion of state-specific trends are reported in the final columns of Table 5. For specifications without state-specific trends, the PH law estimate for wine is essentially the same as the other specifications in terms of magnitude and significance, whereas the estimates for beer, spirits are markedly higher.[66] Also as with the other specifications, once state-specific trends are

[64] For each Northeastern subset specification, the correlation between the fixed effects and the independent variables ranges from .99 to 1.0.

[65] Using 2SLS with a first stage linear probability model produces similar results. Coefficients for wine and beer regressions are negative and significantly larger but those for spirits are insignificant.

[66] For all specifications, tobacco tax has a positive and significant effect on the probability of PH law treatment. For wine, percent democratic has a negative and significant effect on the probability of PH law adoption, whereas for spirits, percent democratic has a positive and significant effect on the

introduced, the estimates becomes smaller and less significant: there is no statistically measurable impact of PH laws on wine or beer consumption, and the estimated impacts of PH laws on spirits and all beverages fall by over half, and 1/3 respectively.

Overall, the results presented in Tables 3-5 provide fairly robust evidence of a causal relationship between PH laws and reduced alcohol consumption. Specifically, the estimates of (1) presented above suggest that PH laws reduce per capita alcohol consumption (measured in gallons of ethanol) by 2-8 percent, with wine and spirits accounting for larger percentage point reductions (8-10 percent) than beer (4-5 percent). This finding may be because beer has much lower alcohol content than wine or spirits, but accounts for the largest share of ethanol consumption, so even large absolute reductions in beer purchases are likely to result in smaller percentage changes. Although the findings are largely statistically significant, they suggest a modest economic impact. Using 2007 national averages, our results imply that consumers in states with PH laws reduce their annual consumption by around 2 bottles of wine, one bottle of spirits, and 2 six-packs of beer a year. Of course, the NIH alcohol per capital measure is based on a denominator of the state population older than 14. In reality, however, only a fraction of the population older than fourteen actually drinks; recent NIH data find that 64% of those over 18 describe themselves as current drinkers,[67] and reported drinking is much less prevalent among those 14-18.[68] Accordingly, the PH laws' impact on per capita assumption among those who consume alcohol is much higher, which suggests that the actual economic effect on this group is also likely to be higher. Further, given the differential impact that PH laws appear to have on wine, beer, and spirits, there are likely second-order welfare losses due to inefficient substitution among different types of alcoholic beverages.

---

probability of PH adoption. Percent democratic is insignificant for beer and all beverages first stage regressions. A Wald test does not reject the hypothesis for independent equations for wine and spirits regressions.

[67] *Percent Distribution of Current Drinking Status*, at
http://www.niaaa.nih.gov/Resources/DatabaseResources/QuickFacts/AlcoholConsumption/dkpat25.htm.

[68] *Trends in Alcohol Use Among 10th Graders*, at
http://www.niaaa.nih.gov/Resources/DatabaseResources/QuickFacts/AlcoholConsumption/dkpat23.htm;
Trends in Alcohol Use Among High School Seniors, at
http://www.niaaa.nih.gov/Resources/DatabaseResources/QuickFacts/AlcoholConsumption/dkpat10.htm.

It is also of interest to note that the tax variables generally are negative and significant across specifications, although the results indicate that the demand for alcohol is inelastic to tax changes: a one percent increase in the average dollar value of alcohol excise taxes will reduce annual per capita alcohol consumption (in gallons of ethanol) by around .05 percent, with wine and spirits being more sensitive to tax changes than beer. Nonetheless, tax policy appears to be a viable lever for reducing average alcohol consumption. Further, the estimated coefficient on wholesaler HHI is negative and significant for the wine regressions (-.04), which is consistent with increased wine and spirit wholesaler concentration at the state level leading to higher consumer prices.

4. The Effects of PH Laws on Social Harms

Ordinarily, laws that suppress competition and reduce output are welfare-reducing. However, when regulation also reduces harmful externalities, it has the potential to produce net benefits. There is a rich empirical literature linking alcohol to a host of social harms, including crime, risky teen behavior, sexually transmitted diseases, and drunk driving.[69] Further, others have found that policies aimed at reducing alcohol consumption have had beneficial effects, for example by reducing crime, binge drinking, or drunk-driving.[70]

The results in the previous section suggest that PH laws work like a tax on alcohol. Several studies have shown a negative relationship between alcohol prices (often measured by excise taxes) and socially harmful behavior. For example, Saffer & Grossman (1987) and Kenkel (1993) report negative relationships between alcohol prices and drunk-driving. Coate & Grossman (1988) find a negative relationship between price and self-reported underage drinking, but this result disappears when religion and other covariates are introduced. More recently, Markowitz & Grossman (1998) find a negative relationship between state beer excise taxes and domestic violence. Accordingly, there are empirically-based reasons to believe that PH laws have the potential to ameliorate external harms associated with alcohol consumption,

---

[69] *See, e.g.*, Conlin et al. (2005); Chesson et al. (2000); Markowitz & Grossman (1998); Dee (2001); Chatterji et al. (2004); Levitt & Porter (2001); Markowitz (2000, 2005).

[70] *See, e.g.*, Carpenter (2007, 2005, 2004); Dee (2001); Eisenberg (2003); Voas et al. (2003).

thus producing benefits that could offset welfare losses due to higher prices. The extent to which PH laws further Twenty-first Amendment concerns, which likely include externalities associated with alcohol consumption, is also germane to legal challenges to PH laws. In this section we examine the relationship between PH laws and two serious social harms associated with alcohol consumption: drunk driving and underage drinking.

4.1   Data and Methodology

We examine the effect of PH laws on social harms using the same basic model as the previous section. Specifically, we estimate the following equation:

$$H_{i,t} = c + \alpha_i + \delta_t + \beta_1 PH_{i,t} + \beta_2 \mathbf{X}_{i,t} + e_{i,t}, \tag{2}$$

where H is one of several measures of social harm: accidents involving at least one driver with an illegal BAC (fatal and non-fatal); self-reported underage drinking and driving; and self-reported underage drinking, including binge drinking. We focus on drunk-driving accidents and underage drinking because they are arguably the most important social harms associated with alcohol sales. In 2008, for example, drunk-driving was responsible for 11,773 deaths – 32% of whom were not the driver. These accidents, moreover, cost an estimated $51 billion annually.[71] Recent years have also witnessed an increased recognition of the deleterious effects of drinking by youth. For example, in 2007 the Surgeon General released a report highlighting the nature and extent of these problems.[72] In addition to injuries and death associated with drunk-driving, underage drinking is a leading contributor to other deaths from other injuries, and is associated with increased risk-taking (including criminal behavior), academic difficulties, developmental problems, and increased risk of future alcohol dependency.

The accident variables are from the National Highway Transportation Safety Administration's (NHTSA) Fatal Accident Reporting Survey (FARS), and are collected annually at the state level. We examine the effect of PH laws on all accidents in which the driver had an illegal BAC, all fatal accidents in which at least one driver had an

---

[71] Centers for Disease Control and Prevention, *Impaired Driving, at*
www.cdc.gov/MotorVehicleSafety/Impared_Driving/imparied-drv_factsheet.htm.

[72] U.S. Dept. of Health & Human Services, The Surgeon General's Call to Action to Prevent and Reduce Underage Drinking (2007).

illegal BAC, and fatal accidents involving a legally drunk driver between 21-34 (the age group responsible for 65% of all fatal drunk-driving accidents).[73] For consistency with the consumption regressions, we use state-level data from 1983-2004. The underage drinking variables are from the Centers for Disease Control's Youth Risk Behavior Surveillance System (YRBSS) annual reports.[74] The YRBSS is a survey of high-school students that occurs every two years. Not all states participate, and participation varies over the sample period. Accordingly, the number of state-year observations ranges from 30-34, and only a core of 13 states report data in every year. These data are available only from 1993.

As in the consumption regressions, the X vector includes demographic, religion, and pricing variables that are likely correlated with alcohol consumption, and thus indirectly correlated with social harms due to alcohol consumption. Also as in the quantity regressions, we also include ZT and BAC08 laws, which are directly aimed at deterring drunk driving. We also include estimated vehicle miles traveled per capita as reported by the Federal Highway Administration for the accident analysis. All regressions using the FARS data include state and year. The YRBSS data provide insufficient within-state variation to identify the PH law effect using a fixed-effects model: only 2 states in the sample (Massachusetts and Delaware) have changed in their PH laws over the relevant time period, only 13 states report every year, and several states appear only once or twice in the data. Accordingly, for the YRBSS regressions we estimate a pooled OLS model with year and census region dummies.

4.2   Results

The results for the FARS regressions are reported in Table 6. The first column in each panel reports specifications that include all three PH laws. Although the beer and spirit coefficients are negative, all are highly insignificant. Because the different PH laws are correlated,[75] the next three columns in each panel report the regression with a dummy variable for only one category of PH law, and again no PH law

---

[73] *See* NHTSA, Traffic Safety Facts 2008.

[74] Carpenter (2004) employs this data at the individual level to measure the effect of zero-tolerance laws on underage behavior.

[75] $\rho_{Spirits,Wine} = .67$; $\rho_{Beer,Wine} = .62$; $\rho_{Beer,Spirits} = .37$.

coefficients are significant. Finally, the last column reports the results from a specification with an indicator variable equal to 1 if a state has any PH law. This estimate is also insignificant. Table 7 reports results from the YRBSS survey data, which are very similar to the FARS results. Although the estimated PH law coefficients are almost uniformly negative, none are statistically distinguishable from zero. The inclusion of national and state-specific trends in other regressions (not reported) yield very similar results.[76]

Although absence of evidence of a PH law effect may not be equivalent to evidence of absence of a PH law effect, it would be difficult to infer from these results that PH laws reduce the drunk driving or underage drinking outcomes that we examine. Unlike the estimated effect of PH laws on consumption – which is almost uniformly negative and significant, and similar in magnitude across various specifications – in the social harms regressions, only 25 out of 42 estimated PH coefficients are negative, and none are statistically significant.

To the extent that PH laws act as a tax, absence of a measurable impact on the drunk driving accidents and teen drinking is inconsistent with some of the prior results discussed above, which find negative relationships between taxes and social harms. One potential reason for this seeming inconsistency may be that earlier work on the relationship between alcohol prices and the harms we measure was based on samples from the 1970s and early 1980s and thus unable to include the effect of ZT and BAC08 laws. Consistent with more recent research [e.g., Carpenter (2004); Dee (2001)], it appears that ZT and BAC08 laws are important sources of reductions in drunk-driving and teen drinking. Specifically, our results suggest that ZT and BAC08 laws reduce alcohol-related accidents by 7-8% and 4-5%, respectively.[77] Further BAC laws appear

---

[76] Because we do not attempt to account for the possible endogeneity of PH laws, these estimates can be considered conservative. If the error term in (2) is positively correlated with the PH treatment decision equation – for example, because states with high levels of drunk driving accidents or underage drinking are more likely to adopt PH laws – then the estimate of the PH law will be biased upward. Additionally, we do not control for possible endogeneity of ZT laws and lower legal BAC laws; because these laws were promoted by the federal government, they can be treated as exogenous, especially since they are not the main variable of interest. Further, the most plausible endogeneity scenario – that states with drunk-driving and underage drinking problems are more likely to adopt ZT and BAC laws – would tend to bias the ZT and BAC coefficients in a positive direction.

[77] The BAC08 results for alcohol-related accidents are in a range similar to those reported by Eisenberg (2003).

to be associated with a 19% reduction in self-reported teen drinking and driving. Surprisingly, we find no apparent effect of ZT laws on teen drinking and driving or binge drinking, but ZT laws are associated with a 4-5% reduction in current teen alcohol use. Another reason for a lack of finding may be that the price increase associated with PH laws is small relative to tax differentials, and thus of insufficient magnitude to change bad behaviors in sufficient magnitude to be statistically measurable. Of course, it is important to note that although the tax variable was negative and often significant in the consumption regressions, it was insignificant in all FARS and YRBSS regressions.

5. Discussion

The results in Sections 3 and 4 suggest that PH laws reduce alcohol consumption but have no measurable effect on two of the most important social ills associated with alcohol – drunk driving accidents and teen drinking. As Cook and Moore (2002, p.122) note, "those in the top decile of the drinking distribution consume more than half of all ethanol. Since alcohol problems are also highly concentrated in this group, it seems reasonable to target alcohol-control policies at them." PH laws do not appear to be very successful in targeting this group. The lack of measurable effect may be because the reduction in consumption is relatively small, leading to only small behavioral changes for those in the top of the alcohol consumption distribution. Further, the consumption effects may be concentrated primarily in the segment of the population that is not likely to engage in the harmful behavior that we examine. Without detailed micro-level data, however, it is impossible to determine the extent to which PH laws had differential effects across the distribution of alcohol consumption.

These results have important legal and policy implications. First, as discussed above, plaintiffs have successfully challenged PH laws on the grounds that they are preempted by the Sherman Act. These results are consistent with the view that PH laws insulate wholesalers from the downward pricing pressure that comes with competition. Unfortunately, data limitations render us unable to determine the relative contributions of concerted versus unilateral behavior to this overall reduction in consumption.

Second, when courts have found PH laws preempted by the Sherman Act, states have attempted – unsuccessfully to date – to take refuge in the Twenty-first Amendment's grant of power to the states to regulate alcohol distribution within their borders by arguing, *inter alia*, that PH laws are designed to "promote temperance." Our results support this contention only in the narrowest sense – if one interprets the Twenty-first Amendment's temperance objective as focused exclusively on reducing average consumption levels *per se* without regard to the social harms associated with consumption. If one takes the view that a societal reduction of alcohol consumption is not a policy goal itself, but rather is valuable primarily as a means to reduce social harms associated with alcohol consumption, our results undercut states' attempts to defend PH laws as legitimate Twenty-first Amendment regulation. Although PH laws reduce average consumption, they appear to have no effect on drunk-driving accidents or the teen drinking behaviors that we examine. Further, even if courts were to accept any reduction in average alcohol consumption as furthering temperance, our results inform the balancing step, where a reduction in non-externality-producing consumption would be weighed against the federal interest in competitive markets.

Third, our findings also cast serious doubt on the wisdom of any proposed legislation that would make challenging these and similar state regulation under the antitrust laws more difficult. Because our results suggest that PH laws reduce consumption without producing a measurable reduction in either drunk driving or underage drinking, antitrust enforcement can play a socially beneficial role by providing a mechanism to eliminate existing PH regimes and to deter states without them from adopting similar laws in the future. Currently proposed legislation seeks to decrease the role of antitrust enforcement by raising the burden of proof facing plaintiffs challenging state regulation of alcohol pricing and distribution and broadening states' ability to defend these regimes under the Twenty-first Amendment.[78] This legislation would likely deter potential plaintiffs from challenging such laws by both increasing the cost of litigation and decreasing the likelihood of success. Our results suggest that constraining antitrust enforcement through the proposed legislation

---

[78] *See, e.g.*, Comprehensive Alcohol Regulatory Effectiveness (CARE) Act, H.R. 5034, 111th Cong. (2010), *available at* http://frwebgate.access.gpo.gov/cgi-bin/getdoc.cgi?dbname=111_cong_bills&docid=f:h5034ih.txt.pdf.

would result in lower consumer welfare for alcoholic beverage consumers with no offsetting reduction in social harms.

Finally, our results indicate that if states desire to reduce alcohol consumption, PH laws appear to be inferior policy instruments relative to feasible alternatives such as enhanced excise taxes; both policies reduce consumption, but the state can return tax revenue to the pubic whereas the supracompetitive prices from PH regimes generate monopoly rents that accrue to wholesalers. Further, policies aimed directly at social harms – such as zero tolerance and BAC reductions – are also superior to PH laws. These policy levers appear to be even more effective than taxes because they reduce harmful behavior without punishing marginal consumers who do not contribute to the targeted social harms.

6. Conclusion

PH laws are one of many sets of regulations that states have enacted since prohibition that limit competition among alcoholic beverage wholesalers. We find that PH laws are associated with lower levels of consumption, but we find no statistically measurable relationship between PH laws and either drunk driving accidents or underage drinking. Taken together, our results suggest a socially beneficial role for antitrust challenges to PH laws and similar anticompetitive state regulation; any policy that would make future challenges more difficult is likely to be harmful. If states wish to reduce the social ills associated with drinking, our results – which are consistent with others – suggest that increasing taxes and enacting laws directly targeting social harms are superior policy instruments to PH laws.

References

Albaek, Svend, Peter Møllgaard, and Per B. Overgaard (1997), "Government-Assisted Oligopoly Coordination? A Concrete Case," *Journal of Industrial Economics* 45: 429, 430, 440.

Baker, Jonathan B. (1996), "Vertical Restraints with Horizontal Consequences: Competitive Effects of "Most Favored-Customer" Clauses," *Antitrust Law Journal* 64: 517.

Carpenter, Christopher (2004), "Heavy Alcohol Use and Youth Suicide: Evidence from Tougher Drunk Driving Laws," *Journal of Policy Analysis and Management* 23(4): 831-842.

Carpenter, Christopher (2005), "Heavy Alcohol Use and the Commission of Nuisance Crime: Evidence from Underage Drunk Driving Laws," *American Economic Review Papers and Proceedings* 95(2): 267-272.

Carpenter, Christopher, Doborah D. Kloska, Patrick O'Malley, and Lloyd Johnston (2007), "Alcohol Control Policies and Youth Alcohol Consumption: Evidence from 28 Years of Monitoring the Future," *The B.E. Journal of Economic Analysis & Policy* 7(1): Article 25 (Topics).

Chatterji, Pinka, Dhaval Dave, Robert Kaestner, and Sara Markowitz (2004) "Alcohol Abuse and Suicide Attempts Among Youth," *Economics and Human Biology* 2: 159-180.

Chesson, Harrell W., Paul Harrison, and William J. Kassler (2000), "Sex Under the Influence: The Effect of Alcohol Policy on Sexually Transmitted Disease Rates in the US," *Journal of Law and Economics* 39: 215-238.

Christensen, Laurits Rolf and Richard E. Caves (1997), "Cheap Talk and Investment Rivalry in the Pulp and Paper Industry," *Journal of Industrial Economics* 45: 47.

Coate, Douglas and Grossman, Michael (1988), "Effects of Alcoholic Beverage Prices and Legal Drink Ages on Youth Alcohol Use," *Journal of Law and Economics*, 31: 145-71.

Conlin, Michael, Stacy Disckert-Conlin, and John Pepper (2005), "The Effect of Alcohol Prohibition on Illicit Drug Related Crimes: An Unintended Consequence of Regulation," *Journal of Law and Economics*, 39: 215-234.

Cook, Philip J. and Moore, Michael J. (2002), "The Economics of Alcohol Abuse and Alcohol-Control Policies," *Health Affairs*, 21(2): 120-32.

Cooper, James C. and Kovacic, William E (2010 *forthcoming*), "U.S. Convergence with International Competition Norms: Antitrust Law and Public Restraints on Competition," Boston University Law Review, 90:101 -149.

Dee, Thomas S. (2001), "Does Setting Limits Save Lives? The Case of 0.08 BAC Laws," *Journal of Policy Analysis and Management* 20(1): 113-130.

Doyle, Maura P. and Christopher M. Snyder (1999), "Information Sharing and Competition in the Motor Vehicle Industry," 107 *Journal of Political Economy* 107: 1326.

Eisenberg, Daniel (2003), "Evaluating the Effectiveness of Policies related to Drunk Driving," *Journal of Policy Analysis and Management* 22(2): 249-274.

Farrell, Joseph (1987), "Cheap Talk, Coordination, and Entry," *RAND Journal of Economics* 18: 34.

Fuller, Stephen W., Fred J. Ruppel, and David A. Bessler (1990), "Effect of Disclosure on Price: Railroad Grain Contracting in the Plains," *Western Journal of Agricultural Economics* 15: 265.

Gillespie, William (1995), "Cheap Talk, Price Announcements, and Collusive Agreements," Department of Justice Economic Analysis Group Working Paper.

Green, Edward, and Robert H. Porter (1984), "Noncooperative Collusion Under Imperfect Price Information," *Econometrica* 52: 87.

Kenkel, Donald S. (1993), "Drinking, Driving, and Deterrence: The Effectiveness and Social Costs of Alternative Policies," *Journal of Law and Economics*, 36(2): 877-913.

Kühn, Kai-Uwe (2001), "Fighting Collusion: Regulation of Communication Between Firms," *Economic Policy* 16(32): 169, 170, 181.

Grossman, Michael and Sara Markowitz (1998), "Alcohol Regulation and Domestic Violence Towards Children," *Contemporary Economic Policy* 16(3): 309-320.

Levitt, Steven D. and Jack Porter (2001), "How Dangerous Are Drinking Drivers?" *Journal of Political Economy* 109: 1198.

Markowitz, Sara J. (2000), "The Price of Alcohol, Wife Abuse and Husband Abuse," *Southern Economic Journal* 67(2): 279-303.

Markowitz, Sara J. (2005) "Alcohol, Drugs, and Violent Crime," *International Review of Law and Economics* 25(1): 20-44.

Møllgaard, H. Peter and Per B. Overgaard (2001) "Market Transparency and Market Power," *Rivista di Politica Economica (Antitrust, Regulation and Competition: Theory and Practice)* 91: 11-58.

Saffer, Henry and Grossman, Michael (1987) "Beer Taxes, The Legal Drinking Age, and Youth Motor Vehicle Fatalities," *Journal of Legal Studies* 16: 351-74.

Salop, Steven C. (1986), "Practices That (Credibly) Facilitate Oligopoly Coordination," in *New Developments in the Analysis of Market Structure,* edited by Joseph E. Stiglitz and G. Frank Matthewson 265-90 (MIT Press).

Sass, T.R. (2005). "The Competitive Effects of Exclusive Dealing: Evidence from the U.S. Beer Industry," *International Journal of Industrial Organization,* 23: 203-225.

Sass, T.R. & Saurman, D.S. (1993). "Mandated Exclusive Territories and Economic Efficiency: An Empirical Analysis of the Malt-Beverage Industry," *Journal of Law and Economics,* 36: 153-77.

Sass, T.R. & Saurman, D.S. (1996). "Efficiency Effects of Exclusive Territories: Evidence from the Indiana Beer Market," *Economic Inquiry,* 34: 597-615.

Schmitz, John and Stephen W. Fuller (1995), "Effect of Contract Disclosure on Railroad Grain Rates: An Analysis of Corn Belt Corridors," *Logistics and Transportation Review* 31: 97.

Scott-Morton, Fiona (1997), "The Strategic Response by Pharmaceutical Firms to the Medicaid Most-Favored-Customer Rules," *RAND Journal of Economics* 28: 269.

Slade, M.E. (1998), "Beer and the Tie: Did Divestiture of Brewer-Owned Public Houses Lead to Higher Beer Prices?," Economic Journal, 108: 1-38.

Stigler, George (1964), "A Theory of Oligopoly," *Journal of Political Economy* 72: 44.

Tirole, Jean (1988), *The Theory of Industrial Organization* (MIT Press).

Viscusi, W. Kip, Joseph E. Harrington, and John M. Vernon (2005), *Economics of Regulation and Antitrust,* 4th Edition, 121-22 (MIT Press).

Vives, Xavier (2002) "Private information, strategic behaviour and efficiency in Cournot markets," *RAND Journal of Economics* 33: 361-376.

Voas, Robert, Scott Tippetts, and James C. Fell (2003), "Assessing the Effectiveness of Minimum Legal Drinking Age and Zero Tolerance Laws in the United States," *Accident Analysis and Prevention* 35: 579-587.

Table 1
Post & Hold Laws: 1983-2010

State	Wine	Beer	Spirits
Connecticut	Y	Y	Y
Delaware	Off in 1999	Y	Off in 1999
Georgia	N	Y	Y
Idaho	Y	Y	N
Maine	Y	Y	N
Maryland	Off in 2004	Off in 2004	Off in 2004
Massachusetts	Off in 1998	Off in 1998	Off in 1998
Michigan	Y	Y	Y
Missouri	Y	N	Y
Nebraska	Off in 1984	N	Off in 1984
New Jersey	Y	Y	Y
New York	Y	N	Y
Oklahoma	Y	Y	Y
Oregon	Off in 1990	Off in 1990	N
Pennsylvania	N	Off in 1999	N
South Dakota	Y	N	Y
Tennessee	N	Y	N
Washington	On in 1995, Off 2008[*]	On in 1995, Off 2008[*]	N
West Virginia	N	N	Y

[*]As a result of a federal appeals court ruing, Washington abandoned their PH laws in 2008.

Table 2
Descriptive Statistics

	Full Sample (n = 1,100)				States With PH Laws During Sample (n = 350)				States Never Adopting PH Laws During Sample (n = 750)			
	$\bar{x}$	σ	Min	Max	$\bar{x}$	σ	Min	Max	$\bar{x}$	σ	Min	Max
Wine	.30	.15	.08	.88	.30	.14	.08	.71	.30	.15	.08	.88
Beer	1.31	.22	.73	2.18	1.20	.13	.91	1.53	1.36	.24	.73	2.18
Spirits	.76	.29	.35	2.45	.73	.20	.35	1.34	.78	.32	.37	2.45
All Beverages	2.37	.56	1.2	5.22	2.23	.34	1.53	3.22	2.44	.62	1.2	5.22
Wine Tax	.64	.53	.01	4.01	.67	.55	.10	4.01	.62	.52	.01	3.02
Beer Tax	.23	.18	.02	1.07	.18	.12	.03	.48	.25	.20	.02	1.07
Spirits Tax	3.16	1.97	.74	15.38	3.4	1.92	.74	10.25	3.05	1.98	.78	15.4
HHI	2432	2370	151	10,000	1859	2033	225	10,000	2699	2469	151	10,000
Per Capita Real Income (000)	22.7	3.8	14.6	32.3	23.2	4.3	16.0	32.3	22.5	3.5	14.6	32.1
% Evangelical	.16	.13	.01	.56	.15	.13	.01	.47	.17	.12	.01	.56
%Catholic	.19	.13	.01	.63	.21	.14	.03	.52	.19	.12	.02	.63
%Married	.47	.04	.40	.60	.47	.04	.41	.60	.46	.04	.40	.59
% White	.82	.12	.23	.99	.83	.09	.64	.99	.81	.13	.23	.99
% < 18	.26	.02	.22	.37	.26	.02	.22	.32				

Table 3
Post & Hold Regressions: All States
(Dependent variable: per capita (age >14) consumption in ethanol equivalent gallons)

	(1)	(2)	(3)	(4)	(5)	(6)
			Wine			
PH	-.09**	-.08*	-.09**	-.09**	-.09**	.01
	(.04)	(.04)	(.03)	(.04)	(.04)	(.02)
R^2	.47	.52	.54	.54	.54	.75
			Beer			
PH	-.02	-.04***	-.05***	-.04***	-.04***	-.04***
	(.02)	(.01)	(.01)	(.01)	(.01)	(.01)
R^2	.30	.57	.58	.59	.59	.81
			Spirits			
PH	-.04	-.10***	-.09**	-.09**	-.09**	-.05**
	(.05)	(.04)	(.06)	(.04)	(.04)	(.02)
R^2	.77	.83	.84	.84	.84	.91
			All Alcoholic Beverages			
PH	-.03**	-.06***	-.06***	-.06***	-.07***	-.03**
	(.02)	(.01)	(.01)	(.01)	(.01)	(.01)
R^2	.64	.80	.80	.80	.80	.89
Demo + Price Factors		Y	Y	Y	Y	Y
Religion			Y	Y	Y	Y
Alcohol Laws				Y	Y	Y
National Trend					Y	
State-Specific Trends						Y

Notes: N= 1,100. Robust standard errors clustered by state in parentheses. *significant at 10% level; **significant at 5% level; ***significant at 1% level. All regressions include state and time effects; price factors includes total tax rates (excise + markup) converted to dollar/gallon equivalents and HHI for wine and spirit wholesalers (variable excluded for beer regressions); demographic variables include real per capita income, percent white, percent married, percent of population under 18; religion variables include percent Evangelical, and percent Catholic; alcohol laws includes MLDA of 21, zero tolerance, and legal BAC limit of .08.

Table 4
Post & Hold Regressions: License States
(Dependent variable: per capita (age >14) consumption in ethanol equivalent gallons)

	(1)	(2)	(3)	(4)
		Wine		
PH	-.09	-.08*	-.08*	.004
	(.06)	(.04)	(.04)	(.02)
R^2	.56	.61	.61	.77
		Beer		
PH	-.02	-.04***	-.05***	-.04***
	(.02)	(.01)	(.01)	(.01)
R^2	.29	.61	.61	.80
		Spirits		
PH	-.04	-.08**	-.08**	-.04*
	(.06)	(.04)	(.04)	(.02)
R^2	.76	.85	.85	.91
		All Alcoholic Beverages		
PH	-.04	-.07***	-.08***	-.03
	(.03)	(.02)	(.01)	(.02)
R^2	.64	.83	.83	.90
Demo + Price Factors		Y	Y	Y
Religion		Y	Y	Y
Alcohol Laws		Y	Y	Y
National Trend			Y	
State-Specific Trends				Y

Notes: N = 704 for all beverages license states; N = 924 for wine license states; N = 704 for spirits license states; N = 1,078 for beer license states. Robust standard errors clustered by state in parentheses. *significant at 10% level; **significant at 5% level; ***significant at 1% level. All regressions include state and time effects; price factors include total tax rates (excise + markup) converted to dollar/gallon equivalents and HHI for wine and spirit wholesalers (variable excluded for beer regressions); demographic variables include real per capita income, percent white, percent married, percent of population under 18; religion variables include percent Evangelical, and percent Catholic; alcohol laws includes MLDA of 21, zero tolerance, and legal BAC limit of .08.

Table 5
Endogenous PH Treatment Regressions
(Dependent variable: per capita (age >14) consumption in ethanol equivalent gallons)

	PH Law States		Northeastern PH Law States		Full Sample MLE	
	(1)	(2)	(3)	(4)	(5)	(6)
	Wine					
PH	-.10***	-.002	-.06***	.01	-.09***	.07
	(.02)	(.02)	(.01)	(.02)	(.02)	(.05)
R^2	.62	.85	.89	.93	-	-
	Beer					
PH	-.04***	-.04***	-.04***	-.01	-.09***	.0003
	(.01)	(.01)	(.01)	(.02)	(.01)	(.02)
R^2	.61	.80	.92	.93	-	-
	Spirits					
PH	-.10**	-.04	-.04**	-.03	-.15***	-.06***
	(.03)	(.03)	(.01)	(.02)	(.04)	(.02)
R^2	.87	.92	.97	.98	-	-
	All					
PH	-.05***	-.02*	-.05***	-.01	-.09***	-.06**
	(.01)	(.01)	(.01)	(.01)	(.04)	(.01)
R^2	.85	.91	.96	.98	-	-
State-specific Trends	Y		Y		Y	

Notes: For wine, PH states and Northeastern PH states, N = 330 and 154, respectively; for beer PH states and Northeastern PH states, N = 286 and 176, respectively; for spirits PH states and Northeastern PH states, N = 264 and 154, respectively; for all PH states and Northeastern PH states, N = 418 and 176, respectively. Full sample maximum likelihood estimation, n = 1,100. Robust standard errors clustered by state in parentheses. *significant at 10% level; **significant at 5% level; ***significant at 1% level; all regressions include state and year fixed effects; total tax rates (excise + markup) converted to dollar/gallon equivalents; HHI for wine and spirit wholesalers (variable excluded for beer regressions); real per capita income, percent white, percent married, percent of population under 18; percent Evangelical, and percent Catholic.

Table 6
Social Harms: Alcohol-Related Automobile Accidents

	Accidents: Driver BAC > .08					Fatal Accidents: Driver BAC > .08					Fatal Accidents Driver Age 21-34: Driver BAC > .08				
	(1)	(2)	(3)	(4)	(5)	(6)	(7)	(8)	(9)	(10)	(11)	(12)	(13)	(14)	(15)
PHWine	.05	.005				.05	.01				.04	.04			
	(.12)	(.04)				(.11)	(.05)				(.15)	(.07)			
PHBeer	-.02		.002			-.02		-.002			.03		.05		
	(.07)		(.05)			(.06)		(.04)			(.08)		(.06)		
PHSpirits	-.07			-.03		-.05			-.02		-.04			.02	
	(.08)			(.04)		(.08)			(.04)		(.14)			(.06)	
PHAny					-.01					-.01					.03
					(.04)					(.04)					(.06)
BAC.08	-.04*	-.04*	-.04*	.04*	-.04*	-.04*	-.04*	-.04*	-.04*	-.04*	-.04	-.04	-.04	-.03	-.04
	(.02)	(.02)	(.02)	(.02)	(.02)	(.02)	(.02)	(.02)	(.02)	(.02)	(.03)	(.03)	(.03)	(.03)	(.03)
ZT	-.07***	-.07***	-.07***	-.07***	-.07***	-.07***	-.07***	-.07***	-.07***	-.07***	-.08***	-.08***	-.08***	-.08***	-.08***
	(.01)	(.02)	(.02)	(.02)	(.02)	(.02)	(.02)	(.02)	(.02)	(.02)	(.03)	(.03)	(.03)	(.03)	(.03)
R^2 (overall)	.74	.74	.74	.74	.74	.74	.74	.74	.74	.74	.81	.81	.81	.81	.81

Notes: N= 1,100. Robust standard errors clustered by state in parentheses. *significant at 10% level; **significant at 5% level; ***significant at 1% level. All regressions include state and time effects and state-specific linear trends. Also included are an indicator for the years in which the MLDA was 21 in state i, and controls for per capita vehicle miles traveled, alcohol tax, real per capita income, percent white, percent married, percent of population under 18; percent Evangelical, and percent Catholic.

Table 7
Social Harms: YRSS Survey Behavior

	Self-Reported Drinking & Driving					Current Alcohol Use					Binge Drinking				
	(1)	(2)	(3)	(4)	(5)	(6)	(7)	(8)	(9)	(10)	(11)	(12)	(13)	(14)	(15)
PHWine	-.16	-.08				-.04	-.03				-.05	-.02			
	(.11)	(.06)				(.04)	(.02)				(.05)	(.03)			
PHBeer	.08		-.02			.01		-.02			-.01		-.02		
	(.08)		(.05)			(.03)		(.02)			(.03)		(.03)		
PHSpirits	.04			-.04		.002			-.02		.07			-.02	
	(.08)			(.06)		(.03)			(.02)		(.05)			(.03)	
PHAny					-.06					-.02					.001
					(.05)					(.02)					(.03)
BAC.08	-.17***	-.18***	-.18***	-.18***	-.19***	-.08***	-.08***	-.08***	-.08***	-.08***	-.11***	-.11***	-.11***	-.11***	-.11***
	(.04)	(.04)	(.04)	(.04)	(.04)	(.02)	(.02)	(.02)	(.02)	(.02)	(.03)	(.04)	(.03)	(.03)	(.03)
ZT	-.02	-.01	-.02	-.02	-.01	-.05*	-.04*	-.04*	-.05*	-.04*	-.03	-.03	-.03	-.03	-.03
	(.05)	(.04)	(.05)	(.05)	(.04)	(.02)	(.02)	(.02)	(.03)	(.02)	(.03)	(.03)	(.03)	(.03)	(.03)
R^2	.79	.79	.78	.78	.78	.83	.80	.80	.80	.83	.79	.78	.78	.78	.78

Notes: N= 193. Robust standard errors clustered by state in parentheses. *significant at 10% level; **significant at 5% level; ***significant at 1% level. All regressions include controls for alcohol tax, real per capita income, percent white, percent married, percent of population under 18; percent Evangelical, and percent Catholic. Regressions also include year dummies and census geographic division dummies.

Table A1
Regression Results for Additional Explanatory Variables in Table 3

	Specifications from Table 3				
	(2)	(3)	(4)	(5)	(6)
	Wine				
TAX	-.06***	-.07***	-.07***	-.07***	-.02
	(.02)	(.02)	(.02)	(.02)	(.02)
HHI	-.04**	-.04**	-.04**	-.04**	-.02
	(.02)	(.02)	(.02)	(.02)	(.03)
EVAN		-.04	-.05	-.05	-.05
		(.06)	(.06)	(.06)	(.05)
CATH		.18	.17	.17	.16
		(.12)	(.12)	(.12)	(.18)
	Beer				
TAX	-.02**	-.02**	-.02**	-.08	-.002
	(.01)	(.01)	(.01)	(.06)	(.03)
EVAN		-.03	-.03	-.02	-.03
		(.03)	(.03)	(.03)	(.03)
CATH		.10*	.11*	.11**	.17**
		(.06)	(.06)	(.05)	(.09)
	Spirits				
TAX	-.05***	-.05***	-.05***	-.05***	-.06**
	(.02)	(.02)	(.02)	(.02)	(.03)
HHI	.01	.01	.01	.01	.002
	(.01)	(.01)	(.01)	(.01)	(.01)
EVAN		.01	.04	.01	-.03
		(.05)	(.04)	(.04)	(.03)
CATH		-.13**	-.09*	-.12*	-.13
		(.06)	(.05)	(.07)	(.12)
	All Alcoholic Beverages				
TAX	-.02	-.02	-.02	-.02	-.02**
	(.02)	(.02)	(.02)	(.02)	(.01)
HHI	.002	.00	.002	.002	.003
	(.01)	(.01)	(.01)	(.01)	(.01)
EVAN		-.03	-.03	-.03	-.07***
		(.03)	(.03)	(.03)	(.03)
CATH		.04	.04	.04	.10
		(.03)	(.04)	(.04)	(.07)

Notes: N= 1,100. Robust standard errors clustered by state in parentheses. *significant at 10% level; **significant at 5% level; ***significant at 1% level.

Table A2
Regression Results for Additional Explanatory Variables in
Table 4

	Specifications from Table 4		
	(2)	(3)	(4)
Wine			
TAX	-.06***	-.06***	-.02
	(.02)	(.02)	(.02)
HHI	-.03	-.03	-.04**
	(.02)	(.02)	(.02)
EVAN	-.10*	-.10*	-.10**
	(.06)	(.06)	(.05)
CATH	.06	.06	-.03
	(.07)	(.07)	(.18)
Beer			
TAX	-.02*	-.08	-.002
	(.01)	(.06)	(.03)
EVAN	-.05*	-.02	-.03
	(.03)	(.03)	(.03)
CATH	.08*	.11**	.17**
	(.04)	(.05)	(.09)
Spirits			
TAX	-.05**	-.05**	-.07*
	(.02)	(.02)	(.04)
HHI	.01	.01	-.01
	(.01)	(.01)	(.01)
EVAN	.01	.01	-.10**
	(.04)	(.04)	(.05)
CATH	-.12*	-.12*	-.31**
	(.07)	(.07)	(.15)
All Alcoholic Beverages			
TAX	-.04**	-.04**	-.002
	(.02)	(.02)	(.02)
HHI	-.01	-.01	.01
	(.01)	(.01)	(.01)
EVAN	-.03	-.03	-.11***
	(.03)	(.03)	(.03)
CATH	.03	.03	-.06
	(.04)	(.04)	(.11)

Notes: N = 704 for all beverages license states; N = 924 for wine license states; N = 704 for spirits license states; N = 1,078 for beer license states. Robust standard errors clustered by state in parentheses. *significant at 10% level; **significant at 5% level; ***significant at 1% level. All regressions include state and time effects;